SCOTLAND
FROM THE AIR

COLIN BAXTER

LOMOND BOOKS

EDINBURGH • SCOTLAND

INTRODUCTION

To fly has always been one of man's great ambitions. Now, at the end of a century of flight, it is still as fascinating as ever to look down on the world from above.

Scotland viewed from the air looks simply amazing. Here is a landscape carved by the glaciers of the last ice age, worn and weathered by wind and rain for over a million years and finally manipulated and manicured by man.

All of these things are graphically illustrated from the air amongst the interplay of light and shadow on the land below. As we travel across Scotland the landscape spreads out like a giant three-dimensional map, a massive jigsaw of shapes, textures and colours. But the intricate details of this grand theatre are equally compelling. The formal planning of Edinburgh's New Town and Glasgow's West End; the tight cluster of dwellings at Europe's best-preserved prehistoric village of Skara Brae on Orkney; the marvellously irregular collection of pools in the blanket bogs of the 'Flow Country' of Caithness; and the fishermen's cottages at Cullen on the Moray coast, huddling together ready for the inevitable cold northeasterly winds.

The photographs in this book take us on a journey around Scotland, over a wide variety of environments. From lowland to highland, city centre to mountain top, coastline and island – an eagle's view of a rich and diverse land.

The journey starts in the Grampian mountains, psychologically central between the west Highlands and the east, and between the far north and the lower lands to the south. In command of the Grampians is the Cairngorm massif, harbouring many of Britain's highest peaks and within which are the great glacial gouges of the Lairig Ghru and Gleann Einich. To the north and east the mountains fade into a vast patchwork of farmland. Castles boldly inspect their estates whilst neatly arranged fishing villages, their harbours growing out of the rock, shelter in folds of the coastline. Aberdeen is the most overgrown of these, bursting with colour, the city centre close behind it, ranks of great grey granite buildings defending invasion by broad-roofed shopping centres. Further south, Dundee spreads out by the Tay estuary, its two long bridges crossing like fine threads to the kingdom of Fife.

Famous for golf, St Andrews also has a long history. The skeleton of its ancient cathedral clings to a corner of the coast, whilst the Old Course drives out to the north on a giant sandy wedge of land. Not far away, distinctive Fife fishing villages, delightful clusters of textured orange pantile roofs, look southwards across the wide expanse of the Firth of Forth.

To the west the Forth Rail Bridge strides across the water, a feat of engineering from the last century alongside the rather less charismatic road bridge. Nearby is the central arena of the capital city, Edinburgh, not so impressive from the air, but the Royal Mile vividly connecting Castle with Palace, and the more regular geometry of the New Town creating green spaces in the midst of all that stone.

We travel further south to the Borders over rolling hills dissected and divided by river, farm and forest. The great Border Abbeys seem to shoot out of the ground. In Dumfriesshire, Caerlaverock Castle still braces itself as a fortress within sight of England.

GLEN AFFRIC (OPPOSITE)

INTRODUCTION

Across the Galloway hills, smothered with forestry, yet with remote hill lochs nestling amid the browns and purples of last year's heather, then west to Ayrshire, where Culzean Castle looks over the sea to the Isle of Arran, surprisingly mountainous above the calm bays below.

Following the Clyde estuary over the islands of Bute and Little Cumbrae, we arrive above Scotland's largest metropolis, Glasgow, more a collection of joined-up small towns than one big city and with plenty of green spaces too. The centre is a guddle, the two arteries of motorway and River Clyde swirling through the confusion, contrasting with the sentinel terraces overlooking Kelvingrove Park and its museum and art gallery.

Westwards we fly across Loch Lomond, deep blue amongst its green islands, to Argyll, which seems more sea than land, more islands than mainland – Jura wild and adrift, Iona a jewel, Staffa and the Treshnish tiny shapes on the edge of the ocean.

Now we are on our way north, looking down on to some of Scotland's most dramatic landscape. Glencoe's mountains are bathed in warm winter light against a sky full of purples with snow-clad Ben Nevis swirling upwards, a dominant mass of rock. Here the Great Glen begins its diagonal thrust through Scotland from Fort William to Inverness. Loch Ness occupies half its length and appears as a huge river, belying its hidden depths.

Heading west again across Lochaber's wonderful hill country draped in autumn's golden browns to the isles of Muck, Eigg, Canna and Rum which seem to float between sky, sea and cloud. The Cuillin hills of Skye loom darkly ahead, a mass of fused mountains more alpine than Scottish, except for the views they command. The island's new bridge leaps across the narrow Kyle Akin, a controversial but permanent attachment to the mainland.

Yet further westwards over Trotternish and across the Minch to a different land – the Western Isles, with glorious white beaches which sweep gracefully at the edge of the Atlantic and where the Standing Stones of Calanais on Lewis reveal a cross shape drawn 5000 years ago.

Back to the mainland and Wester Ross, a myriad of mountains, lochs and offshore islands. Across Sutherland to the wild north coast, and yet more islands. We sample Orkney: the reds of Hoy's battered cliffs, the dome of Maes Howe burial chamber, and Stromness quiet in its natural harbour.

Now it is time to journey south again, down a coastline decorated with castles and the deserted remains of crofts and brochs. Long bridges span wide firths, a golf course sits wedged between beaches and we find ourselves at the other end of the Great Glen looking down on the River Ness, winding through Inverness into the Moray Firth.

Finally we travel over green straths back to the heart of the Grampians. Snow cloaks the busy northern slopes of the Cairngorms and the rising sun carves pink corries out of the land, reminding us of its formation by the ice all that time ago, and heralding a new day across Scotland.

Colin Baxter

'...a landscape carved by the glaciers of the last ice age, worn and weathered for over a million years...'

THE CAIRNGORMS — THE LAIRIG GHRU (OPPOSITE), NORTHERN CORRIES (LEFT), GLEANN EINICH (RIGHT).

7

PORTSOY, ABERDEENSHIRE (LEFT);
DOVECOT, BARNYARDS OF FINDLATER,
ABERDEENSHIRE (ABOVE).

SEATOWN, CULLEN, MORAY.

9

THE RIVER DEVERON AT SCATTERTIE, ABERDEENSHIRE.

FYVIE CASTLE, ABERDEENSHIRE.

11

ABERDEEN CITY CENTRE AND HARBOUR.

STONEHAVEN HARBOUR AND THE EAST COAST LOOKING TOWARDS DUNNOTTAR CASTLE.

THE RIVER DEE AT MUIR OF DINNET, ABERDEENSHIRE

BRAEMAR AND THE RIVER DEE, ABERDEENSHIRE

BLAIR CASTLE, PERTHSHIRE.

Ben Lawers and Loch Tay.

THE TAY BRIDGES AND FIRTH OF TAY.

THE DISCOVERY CENTRE, DUNDEE (ABOVE);
DUNDEE CITY AND THE TAY BRIDGE (RIGHT).

St Andrews Cathedral and Town (left);
St Andrews Golf Courses (opposite).

Fields of rape, Fife.

22

LOCH LEVEN CASTLE, KINROSS.

LEVEN LINKS, LARGO BAY, FIFE.

PITTENWEEM, FIFE.

WALLACE MONUMENT, STIRLING.

THE RIVER FORTH AT STIRLING.

ABOVE THE FORTH BRIDGES, LOOKING WEST.

28

THE FORTH BRIDGE AND FIRTH OF FORTH;
LOOKING EAST (ABOVE) AND LOOKING NORTH (RIGHT).

MORAY PLACE AND AINSLIE PLACE, NEW TOWN, EDINBURGH.

EDINBURGH CASTLE AND
THE ROYAL MILE.

MELROSE ABBEY, BORDERS.

FORESTRY NEAR LIDDESDALE, BORDERS.

PEEBLES, BORDERS.

TRAQUAIR HOUSE, NEAR INNERLEITHEN (ABOVE LEFT); AND THE RIVER TWEED (ABOVE RIGHT), BORDERS.

CAERLAVEROCK CASTLE, DUMFRIESSHIRE (OPPOSITE); DUMFRIES AND THE RIVER NITH (ABOVE).

37

SWEETHEART ABBEY, NEW ABBEY,
DUMFRIESSHIRE.

38

LOCH ENOCH, GALLOWAY HILLS.

CULZEAN CASTLE, AYRSHIRE.

TURNBERRY GOLF COURSE, AYRSHIRE.

Lamlash, Isle of Arran (left);
Brodick Castle, Isle of Arran
(opposite)

LITTLE CUMBRAE, FIRTH OF CLYDE.

44

ROTHESAY CASTLE, ISLE OF BUTE.

PARK CIRCUS AND PARK QUADRANT, KELVINGROVE, GLASGOW.

GLASGOW MUSEUM AND ART GALLERY, KELVINGROVE.

M8 MOTORWAY AT TOWNHEAD, GLASGOW (ABOVE LEFT); GEORGE SQUARE, GLASGOW (ABOVE RIGHT).

THE RIVER CLYDE AND GLASGOW CITY CENTRE.

49

LOCH LOMOND.

ERSKINE BRIDGE AND THE RIVER CLYDE.

INVERARAY AND LOCH FYNE, ARGYLL (LEFT);
THE 'HEBRIDEAN PRINCESS' AT CRINAN,
ARGYLL (ABOVE).

THE SOUND OF JURA.

IONA AND THE ROSS OF MULL.

Staffa, Little Colonsay and Ulva, with the Treshnish Isles and Tiree in the distance.

EASDALE ISLAND, ARGYLL.

OBAN, ARGYLL.

LOCH ETIVE AND BEN STARAV (ABOVE); GLENCOE (OPPOSITE).

58

Ben Nevis (opposite);
Aonach Mór, near
Fort William (right).

FORT AUGUSTUS AND LOCH NESS.

LOCH NESS, THE GREAT GLEN.

LOCH HOURN, LOCHABER.

64

'THE SMALL ISLES' OF MUCK, CANNA, RUM AND EIGG.

The Cuillin Hills, Isle of Skye (opposite); The Skye Bridge and Loch Alsh (above).

DUNVEGAN CASTLE, ISLE OF SKYE.

THE STORR, TROTTERNISH, ISLE OF SKYE.

Tràigh na Berie, Kyles Pabay and Pabay Mór, Isle of Lewis.

CALANAIS STANDING STONES, ISLE OF LEWIS.

LOCH TORRIDON, WESTER ROSS.

LOCH MAREE, WESTER ROSS.

SUMMER ISLES.

ULLAPOOL, LOCH BROOM, WESTER ROSS.

'THE FLOW COUNTRY' OF CAITHNESS (OPPOSITE);
INVERNAVER, TORRISDALE BAY,
SUTHERLAND (ABOVE AND RIGHT).

Skara Brae prehistoric village, Mainland, Orkney (left); Maes Howe burial tomb, Mainland, Orkney (above).

STROMNESS, MAINLAND, ORKNEY.

THE BERRY, HOY, ORKNEY (ABOVE); THE OLD MAN OF HOY, ORKNEY (OPPOSITE)

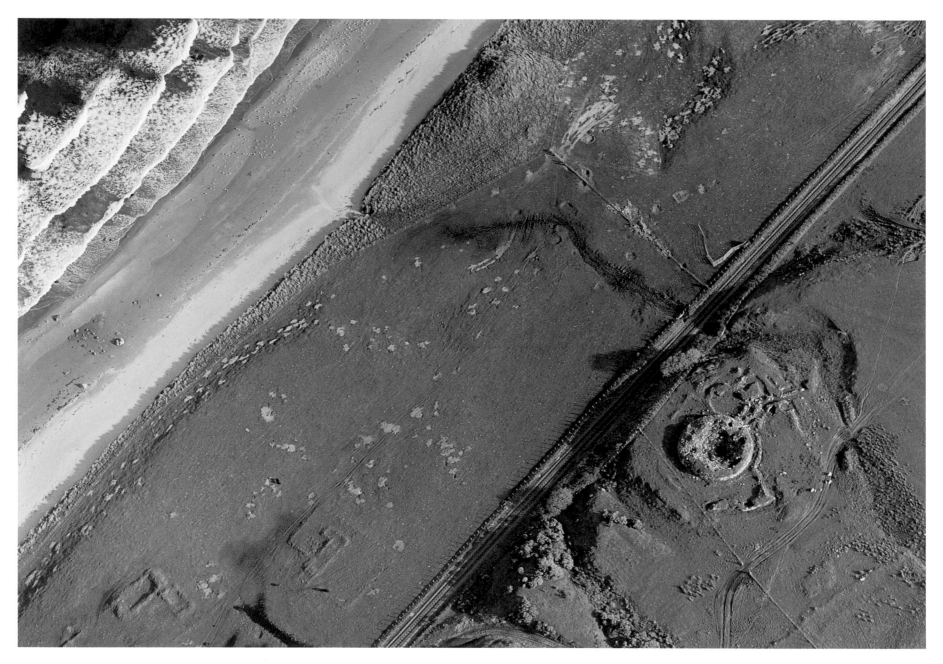

Broch, railway and beach near Ballinreach on the east coast of Sutherland.

STACKS OF DUNCANSBY, CAITHNESS.

DORNOCH BRIDGE AND
DORNOCH FIRTH (OPPOSITE);
DUNROBIN CASTLE NEAR
GOLSPIE, SUTHERLAND (RIGHT).

FORT GEORGE, MORAY FIRTH.

CHANONRY POINT, MORAY FIRTH.

INVERNESS, THE RIVER NESS AND MORAY FIRTH.

KESSOCK BRIDGE AND BEAULY FIRTH.

STRATHNAIRN, INVERNESS-SHIRE.

URQUHART CASTLE AND
LOCH NESS, INVERNESS-SHIRE.

Northern Corries of the Cairngorms – Lurcher's Gully (above left); Coire Cas (above right).

92

LOCH MORLICH AND THE CAIRNGORM MOUNTAINS.

COIRE GARBHLACH (ABOVE) AND BRAERIACH AT DAWN (RIGHT), CAIRNGORMS.

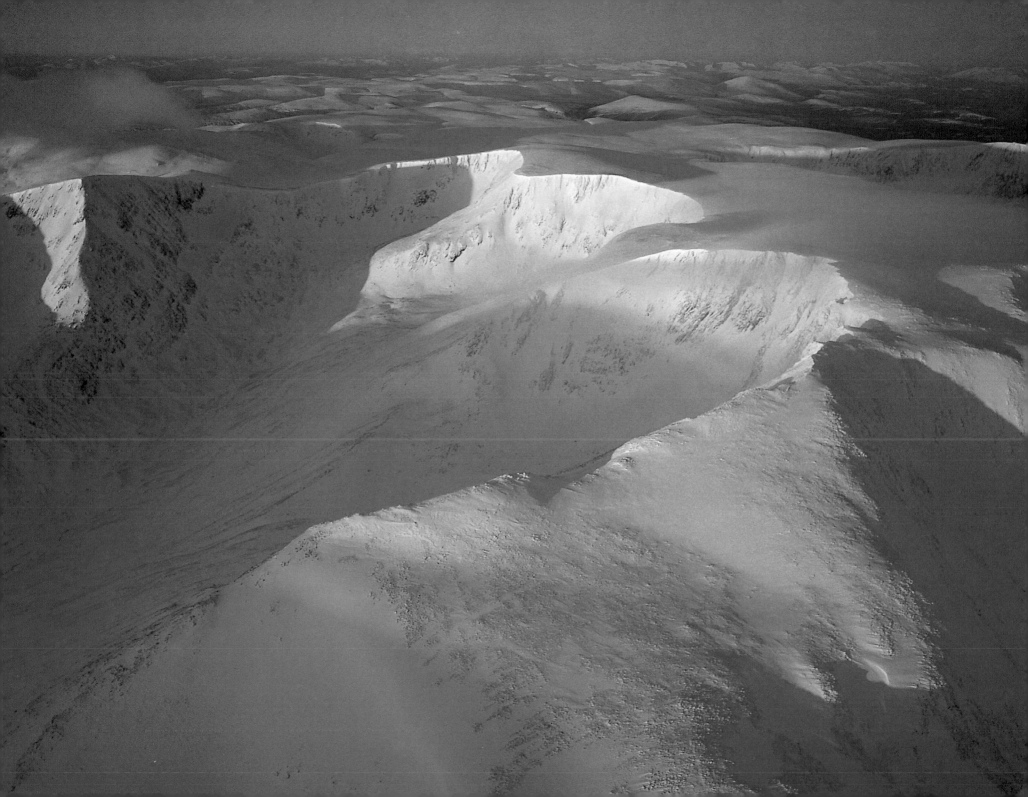

Index of Places

First published in hardback in Great Britain in 1997 by
Lomond Books, 36 West Shore Road, Granton, Edinburgh EH5 1QD
Reprinted 1998, 1999, 2000

Revised Paperback Edition first published in 2002
Reprinted 2003, 2004
Produced by Colin Baxter Photography Ltd.

Photographs and Text Copyright © Colin Baxter 1997, 2002, 2003, 2004
All rights reserved

ISBN 1-84204-044-8   Printed in China
Front cover photograph: The Forth Bridge and the Firth of Forth; Page 1 photograph: Anstruther Easter, Fife
Back cover photographs: Balmoral Castle and the River Dee; The West Coast of Harris, Western Isles; Pittenweem, Fife.